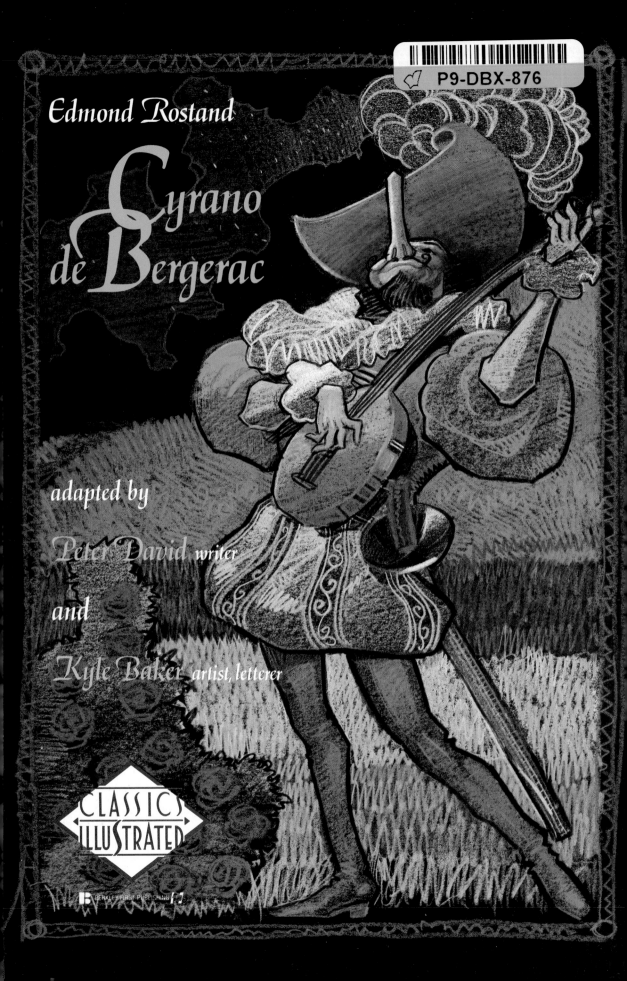

Edmond Rostand

Cyrano de Bergerac

adapted by

Peter David writer

and

Kyle Baker artist, letterer

CLASSICS
ILLUSTRATED

BERKLEY FIRST PUBLISHING

Edmond Rostand's immortal fame rests upon a sole literary work — **Cyrano de Bergerac**. The five-act verse drama was Rostand's fourth play, following his successful *La Princess Lointaine* (1895). At the time, his prominence was waxing and his influence was growing; popular theatrical stars of the period — including Sarah Bernhardt — vied for roles in Rostand's plays. **Cyrano de Bergerac** (1898) was an immediate and enormous triumph. The witty production was a radical departure from the drama of the period, and represented Rostand's attempt to revive romance in place of the realistic conventions that had pervaded the theatre. The play's hero, Cyrano, an aspiring poet and lover, is based upon a homely soldier and writer who lived during the early seventeenth century. Rostand used Cyrano — a gallant and radiant soul cursed with an unattractive face — to symbolize magnanimity, and the beauty of the inner soul. A masterful blend of comedy, tragedy, and romance, **Cyrano de Bergerac** has touched and thrilled audiences since it was first staged. Of Rostand's six plays, it alone has endured through the years. The enchanting, bittersweet melodrama remains one of the best-loved plays in the history of the theatre.

Cyrano de Bergerac
Classics Illustrated, Number 21

Wade Roberts, Editorial Director   Kurt Goldzung, Creative Director
Mike McCormick, Art Director   Valarie Jones, Editor

PRINTING HISTORY
1st edition published March 1991

For information, address: First Publishing, Inc., 435 North LaSalle St., Chicago, Illinois 60610.

ISBN 0-425-12528-9

Distributed by Berkley Sales & Marketing, a division of The Berkley Publishing Group, 200 Madison Avenue, New York, New York 10016.

Printed in the United States of America
1 2 3 4 5 6 7 8 9 0

Such, my dear sir, is what you **might** have said, if you had wit or were a man of letters. But of wit, sir, you never had an atom. And of letters, you need only **three** to describe you: A...S...S!

Scoundrel! Lout! Fool!

You're aptly named. And I am Cyrano Savinien Hercule de Bergerac... and, by happy fortune, my sword was just feeling cramped from **inactivity**.

But I need **mental** exercise as well as physical.

So, while we battle, I shall compose a **poem**, and at its conclusion, **stab** you. Now let's see... what to rhyme, what to...

Look **out**!

Give room!

Ah! Yes. **Here** we go.

"Gracefully I toss my hat, And doff my splendid cape..."

"I carefully remove my sword From scabbard, hear it scrape? Glorious as Scaramouche Or Lancelot, in his day, I warn you now, my French 'Hors D'Oeuvre' At poem's end - - Touché.

"Better you had fled this fight, A well-cooked goose are you. How best to serve you up? Au jus? Or mayhap cordon bleu? A roasted rump? No, no! Of course! A pork belly today. I'll carve you up, like common swine, At poem's end - - Touché.

Silence him, Valvert!

So Cyrano **did** show up! I knew he would, the patronless fool.

I **fear** for him, Le Bret!

Good heavens, **why?** He's **safest** when he's fighting.

"How now? You run? I'll make my point-
Deflecting yours. Now fight!
A coward's yellow suits your skin,
Though now you're sickly white.
A ghostly hue, a ghostly you
I'll exorcise away.
The fate you planned for me is yours,
At poem's end-- Touché."

Refrain:
"Apologize to God, dear sir,
And for your soul, I'll pray.
Your short engagement's
at an end...

"At poem's end - - Touché!"

Superb!

Wonderful!

The best show in **ages!**

Madman.

You're **insane**, Cyrano! You make enemies right and left, you have no patron, no nobleman to protect you. . .

. . . and no funds, for you threw your entire month's wages into the crowd! You have no money!

Ah, but I have **style**, Le Bret, which is **beyond** price. What a gesture, eh?

First, dearest cousin, I must thank you for checkmating that foolish Viscount de Valvert last night in swordplay. He is a follower of De Guiche, a nobleman who rather **aggressively** seeks my favor. You taught **him** a lesson, Cyrano, and mayhap in so doing, **De Guiche** as well.

Then I am happy as well, Roxanne... as happy as that blessed moment when you remembered that I humbly exist, and asked to meet me.

Oh, how could I **ever** forget you? My childhood friend, almost as a **brother** to me. Every spring we would come to Bergerac and play by the lakeside.

Little Roxanne in her short frock.

Was I **fair** then?

You were not foul. But come... what did you wish to tell me?

Dear Cyrano... I am in **love!**

Ah.

But with one who knows **not**. At least, not **yet**.

Ah.

A poor youth who all this time has loved **timidly** from afar, and dares not speak, yet I have seen love **trembling** on his lips!

Ah.

A soldier in **your** regiment.

Ah.

In your own **company**.

Ah.

He is proud, noble, intrepid...

Cyrano! Our entire regiment, and all the fashionable people in Paris, have come to hear of your great **victory** last night!

Who told them I was here?!

I did, of course!

Cyrano! **There** he is! It's **Cyrano!**

Cyrano! My friend! My **friend!**

Odd. I did not have all these friends yesterday.

Look! It's Count De Guiche!

The Marshal of Gassion expresses his admiration of your widely proclaimed exploit, sir. Likewise, my uncle, the Cardinal Richelieu, fancies you.

Tell me, my dear poet and playwright... what think you of **me** as your **patron?**

Seriously?

Oh, yes. For example, your play "Agrippine" would at last be staged... after I have **rewritten** some of it, of course.

I see! If you cannot **beat** me, **enjoin** me!

What would you **have,** sir? That I wrap myself around the protecting tree of a patron, like crawling ivy? Not **I!** Dedicate verses to bankers, and cringe in hopes of seeing my patron smile my way? Not **I!**

Be terrorized by all, and terrorizing to none? Not **I!** Grow pale and calculating, seeking introductions and accepting contradictions, give up all that I am to become one whom I would detest? Not I, I say, and again, **not** I!

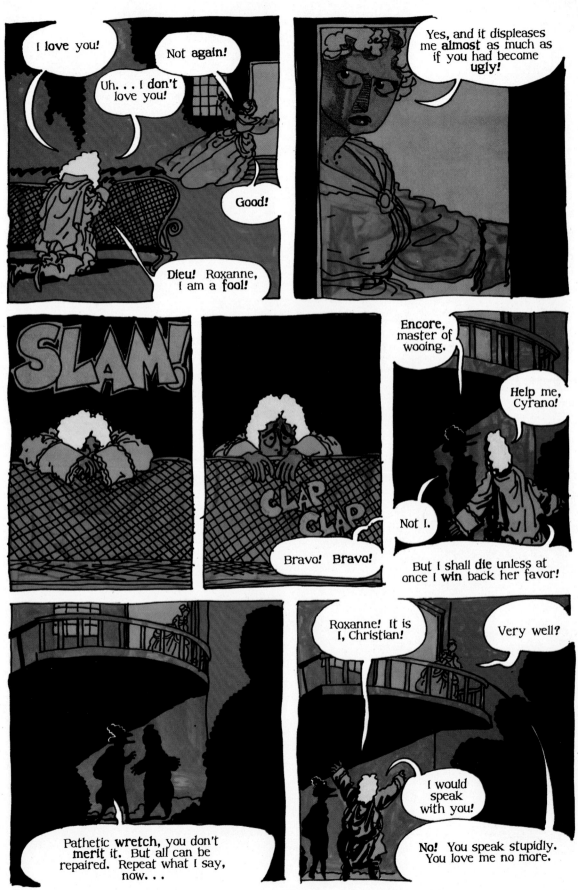

Good sir, is this the house of Roxanne Robin?

Yes, good friar. Why?

Ah. Miss Robin. I bring a letter from Count De Guiche. The contents, I confess, are unknown to me, but are quite **urgent**.

Lord! It says De Guiche is coming to marry me, in a service performed by this friar! And a man of his power will **not** be denied!

But he **can** be thwarted . . . thusly. . .

Good friar. This note says that I am to give you two hundred gold pieces and that you are to marry me to the Count de Neuvil here.

But the note says - -

Shut **up**, Christian.

Two hundred **gold** pieces for the church! Prepare for **marriage**, my child.

Cyrano! Stall De Guiche, **whatever** it takes!

What's **this?!** Where fell that man from?

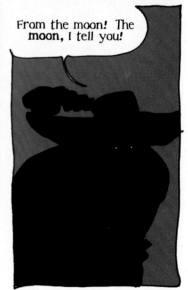

From the moon! The **moon**, I tell you!

27

29

"My dearest love -- the war here passes slowly. Our greatest enemies are the Spanish, and hunger.

"But such hunger is a trifle...

"...Compared to the hunger that I, your Christian, feel in my soul for you..."

Sirs, I hear that in your ranks you **scoff** at me, your **Colonel!** Only uneducated mountain **louts** such as you would hold **me** in disdain.

Not true, sir. The Spanish **also** hold you in disdain.

I can ignore your taunts. 'Tis well known how I bear me in the war. Why, yesterday my **own** men beat back the Count of Bucquoi, after **three** separate charges.

I heard about that. When you were **beset** by the enemy, you **tossed away** your white scarf of rank, to make it that much easier for you to **run away**.

In **my** opinion, King Henry IV would not have, no matter the **odds**, stripped himself of **his** white helmet plume.

But I lived to **attack** again! The ruse succeeded.

Mayhap. But the white plume, or scarf, signifies the honor of being a **target**. One does not lightly abdicate that honor.

Why, if you lent me your scarf, I **would**, this very night, wear it **myself** and lead **assault** against the enemy.

Another Gascon boast! You **know** the scarf now lies in enemy territory. No one could fetch it hither and **live!**

Here it is.

You retrieved it this morning, didn't you? While making **another** of your mad dawn dashes to post a letter to Roxanne. You'll be **killed**.

He sleeps. How pale he is, but how handsome **still**, despite his **sufferings**. If his poor little lady-love knew that he is **dying** of hunger...

You **know** it is the Spanish custom to **shoot** at me every morning and **miss**. Besides, I **promised** he should write often.

I have **news** for you. Last evening, the Marshal set out for Dourlens, in a **desperate** effort to obtain us needed supplies. But in so doing, he took **half** the army with him.

So we are to gain time until the Marshal returns?

Yes, by being **good** enough to get ourselves **killed**. And our **Colonel** will be **departing** before that time, of course.

Do the **Spaniards** know?

Aye, they know. And they will **attack** us, likely within the hour.

Of course.

I know you **love** to fight against five score, Cyrano. You will not **now** complain of paltry odds.

Roxanne... at least, if I could send my heart's **farewell** to her in a fair letter...!

I had prepared for this. **Here** is your letter.

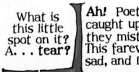 What is this little spot on it? A. . . tear?

 **Ah!** Poets sometimes get so caught up in their false emotions, they mistake them for truth. This farewell letter was passing sad, and I wept while writing it.

Wept? **Why?**

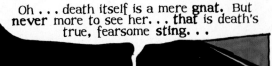 Oh . . . death itself is a mere **gnat.** But **never** more to see her. . . **that** is death's true, fearsome **sting**. . .

 A carriage! A **carriage** is coming!

 On the king's service! We come on the king's **service!**

 **You?!** On the king's service?

How did you **find** us?!

 What greater king is there than **love?** As for finding you. . .

I followed the trail of a country laid waste. What **horrors!** If such be the services of **your** king, I would fainer serve **mine.**

Now, tell me **why** you risked such **danger** to come hither.

Why, your **letters** brought me here! They turned my head - - so **many**, and **each** one more **beautiful** than the one before!

What? For a few inconsequential love letters - - !

Each separate page was like a fluttering flower petal, loosed from **your** own soul and wafted thus to **mine**. Each word **burning** with sincerity.

You **really** felt such **sincere** love. . . ?

Oh, **yes!** And with **death** so close, I have come to **beg** you to **forgive** me for the insult done to you. For I, frivolous, at first loved you only for your **face!**

But I did you **such** injustice! For **now**, it is for your **soul** that I truly love you. I should love you even if your beauty were to **depart.**

No! Don't say that!

It's **true!** I care **not** about your face! I would love you even if you were **ugly!**

No! Not that!

Please, God, not **that!**

His victory **overwhelms** him.

34

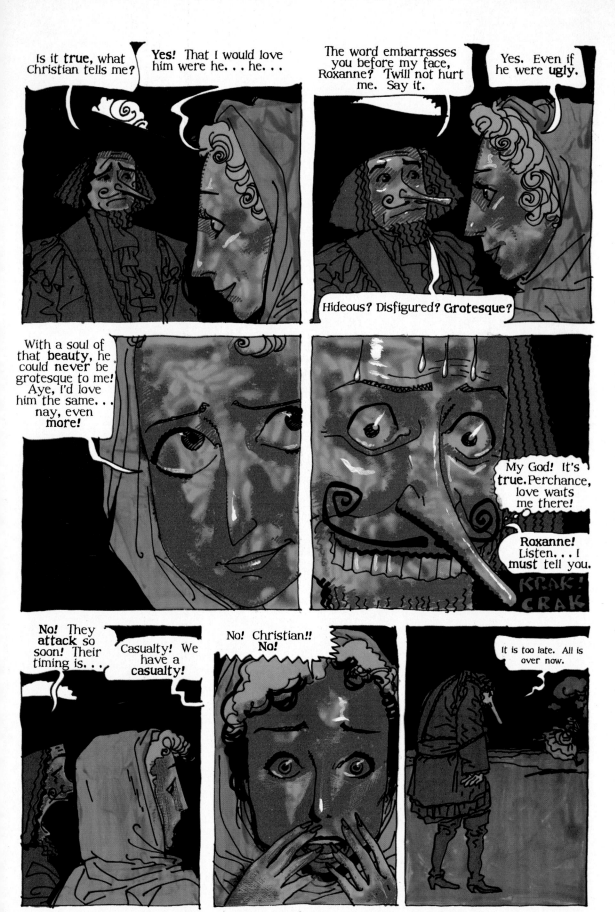

The Marshall indeed returned in time, and the day was won... but not without many deaths. Cyrano survived. He could not, however, betray the dying belief of his friend, nor tarnish his memory. And so he kept silent... for fifteen years.

Here he comes.

His sword will not reach **here**, methinks.

Compliments of an **admirer**, Monsieur de Bergerac.

And so you stayed here in this convent all these years, Roxanne? Still beautiful, and. . . **still** in mourning?

And **dead**, you love him **still?**

Yes, dear Count. . . pardon, **Duke**. . . De Guiche. **Still** in mourning. And I carry **always** Christian's last letter next to my **heart**.

At times, Le Bret, it seems he is but **partly** dead. Our **hearts** still speak, as if his **love**, still warm, **wrapped** itself around me.

Does Cyrano come to see you?

Oh, yes, **often**. He mocks my tapestry that's never done, and tells me gossip of the week. We call him my "gazette."

Cyrano lives alone, in **poverty**, just as I predicted. His writings make him fresh enemies. And yet, I fear for him, **not** man's attack, but solitude, hunger, cold December days.

Pity him **not!** He has lived out his vows, **free** in his thoughts and actions. Uncompromising.

I have **all**, and he has **naught**. . . yet, I would be **proud** to shake his hand.

Le Bret. . . when you next see Cyrano. . . tell him that I heard at card play yesterday someone say, "That Cyrano, he may die. . . by accident." **Warn** him to stay home for a time.

The years have made you **wise**, Duke. Good day, gentlemen.

I shall go **straight** to his home and tell him. Thank you, Monsieur.

Heavens! The late Cyrano de Bergerac!

Yes. . . late, for the first time in all these years. I was delayed. . . by an **unwelcome** visitor. A creditor. . . with a debt to claim.

I told him I had a standing rendezvous. . . and that he should return in an hour's time.

He can wait! I shall **not** let you go 'ere twilight falls.

I think that is just about when I shall be leaving you.

The usual. The king over-ate and fell ill, but is now recovered. The court traveled here and there. And on today, Saturday, the twenty-sixth. . .

That tapestry. . . there will be an end to me before an end of it.

I **knew** you'd make some joke. So . . . tell me what news there is in court.

Cyrano! What's **wrong**?

Tis **nothing**. That old wound, from the war, sometimes. . . see? It passes now.

Each of us has his wound. Aye, I have **mine**. Tis **here**, beneath this letter, brown with age, stained with **teardrops** and **blood**.

You **promised** one day you would let me read it. Today, if you please.

40

"Roxanne, adieu. I am to die this very night, beloved, and my soul is heavy with unspoken love. No longer will my eyes be able to feast upon you, to treasure your least gesture. The way your hand flutters to your face as you speak, or gently brush back your hair. So, too, do I wish you could brush back death, so that my heart would not have to cry out, farewell, my love!"

How you **read** that letter. One would **think**...

"My life departs, and yet you, my life, will remain. My life, my love, my sweetest jewel..."

You read in such a voice... **strange**, and yet... **familiar**...

"Here I die, and as I enter heaven will cast down my heart to you, to leave it with you so that you may know..."

How **can** you read? It is too **dark**.

"... that it was I who loved you, beyond measure..."

Oh, dear **God!**

"... beyond reason, beyond hope..."

And all these years, you've played the part of the kind old **friend** who comes to laugh and chat!

...I never... loved... you...

Twas **you!**

No! **Never!** Roxanne, **no!**

No, **Roxanne!**

All the letters, the sweet, mad-love words-- **you!**

The voice in the night, **yours!**

I **swear** to you, no!

The soul - - it was **your** soul!

Twas **his!**

You loved me!

No! No, my sweet love - -

The tears on the letter... **your** tears...

The blood was **his.**

Why **now** break this noble silence? Why **today?**

I **knew** it! **Here** he is!

He was taken to his bed injured, Madame! He has ensured his **death** by coming here!

Ah, yes. My **death.** To conclude my gazette: On Saturday, the twenty-sixth. . .

Monsieur de Bergerac was assassinated. Did I die **nobly,** sword in hand? **Nay!** Killed in an **ambush,** at the hand of a lackey! 'Tis very well. My **death** is as great a **failure** as my **life.**

Live, for I **love** you!

Ah**!** In **fairy** tales, the lady says "I love you" to the beast, and all his ugliness **fades** fast. But see? I remain the **same.**

I have **ruined** your life! I**!**

You? You **blessed** my life! Thanks to your friendship, my existence has been blessed by a woman's charm.

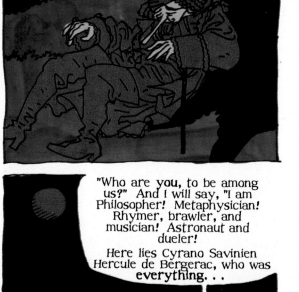

I've **loved** only one man, ever, and now I have **lost** him **twice.**

De Guiche. . . I shall soon reach the moon with no projectile's aid. **There** shall be my Paradise, and I shall find the lost souls that I love. The philosophers. And they will look at me and say. . .

"Who are **you,** to be among us?" And I will say, "I am Philosopher! Metaphysician! Rhymer, brawler, and musician! Astronaut and dueler!

Here lies Cyrano Savinien Hercule de Bergerac, who was **everything.** . .

. . .and **nothing.**"

Do not mourn **less** for Christian, my love... I but ask that when my body is cold as clay, you mourn a **bit** for me as well.

I **swear** to you, I --

Now, wait! He **comes!** But I'll **not** meet him this way! Not seated, **no!**

He's **delirious!**

I shall meet death on foot, sword in hand!

What!? He **dares** to mock my nose! Ho, insolence!

Useless to fight you? I do not **need** hope for success to fight! I am **champion** of **lost** causes and **fruitless quests!**

You there! Who **are** you?

Of course! You are legion, but I know every one of your names! My old **enemies!**

Edmond Rostand's immortal fame rests upon a sole literary work — **Cyrano de Bergerac**. The five-act verse drama was Rostand's fourth play, following his successful *La Princess Lointaine* (1895). At the time, his prominence was waxing and his influence was growing; popular theatrical stars of the period — including Sarah Bernhardt — vied for roles in Rostand's plays. **Cyrano de Bergerac** (1898) was an immediate and enormous triumph. The witty production was a radical departure from the drama of the period, and represented Rostand's attempt to revive romance in place of the realistic conventions that had pervaded the theatre. The play's hero, Cyrano, an aspiring poet and lover, is based upon a homely soldier and writer who lived during the early seventeenth century. Rostand used Cyrano — a gallant and radiant soul cursed with an unattractive face — to symbolize magnanimity, and the beauty of the inner soul. A masterful blend of comedy, tragedy, and romance, **Cyrano de Bergerac** has touched and thrilled audiences since it was first staged. Of Rostand's six plays, it alone has endured through the years. The enchanting, bittersweet melodrama remains one of the best-loved plays in the history of the theatre.

Cyrano de Bergerac
Classics Illustrated, Number 21

Wade Roberts, Editorial Director
Mike McCormick, Art Director

Kurt Goldzung, Creative Director
Valarie Jones, Editor

PRINTING HISTORY
1st edition published March 1991

For information, address: First Publishing, Inc., 435 North LaSalle St., Chicago, Illinois 60610.

ISBN 0-425-12528-9

Distributed by Berkley Sales & Marketing, a division of The Berkley Publishing Group, 200 Madison Avenue, New York, New York 10016.

Printed in the United States of America
1 2 3 4 5 6 7 8 9 0